STORYTELLING FOR THE DEFENSE

THE DEFENSE ATTORNEY'S COURTROOM GUIDE TO BEATING PLAINTIFFS AT THEIR OWN GAME

Merrie Jo Pitera, Ph.D. & Barbara Hillmer, Ph.D.

INDIE BOOKS
INTERNATIONAL

ISBN-10: 1-941870-41-4
ISBN-13: 978-1-941870-41-9
Library of Congress Control Number: 2015947903

The Eight-Step Persuasive Story Methodology™ is a trademark of Litigation Insights
Ford Pinto is a registered trademark of the Ford Motor Company.
Pacific Gas and Electric Company is a registered trademark of the PG&E Corporation.
Dole is a registered trademark of the Dole Food Company, Inc.
Chevron is a registered trademark of the Chevron Corporation.
ELMO is a registered trademark of the ELMO COMPANY, LIMITED.

The use of product names in this book does not indicate that the listed companies
are a sponsor, affiliate or endorser of this book or Litigation Insights.

Designed by Joni McPherson, mcphersongraphics.com

INDIE BOOKS INTERNATIONAL, LLC
2424 VISTA WAY, SUITE 316
OCEANSIDE, CA 92054
www.indiebooksintl.com

TABLE OF CONTENTS

SECTION III
The Power of Improved Jury Connection

ABOUT THE AUTHORS

FOREWORD

Stories capture our imagination. They resonate with us because they feel familiar. Ever since we were little children we learned from stories, fables, fairy tales and myths. Storytelling also creates opportunities to use analogies and metaphors to make points that draw parallels to broader human experience. An effective advocate is a good storyteller, whether presenting a case in the courtroom or representing a client in a negotiation or a mediation.

In a jury trial, a case is most persuasive when presented as a storytelling narrative based on compelling themes. Successful plaintiffs' lawyers know this. They also understand that the presentation of a case needs to have emotional as well as intellectual appeal in order to engage the members of a jury. Most people, including jurors, make decisions based on their emotional feelings about what seems right, or desirable, or fair. They then use rational arguments to justify to themselves and to other people the decisions they have already made. They seldom use logical analysis to reason to a conclusion when they make decisions in the affairs of life.

All too often defense lawyers neglect their storytelling skills and avoid addressing the emotional content of a case. They take refuge in chronological presentations of factual information and logical arguments based on the legal elements of the claims and defenses in the case. That approach may seem rational and compelling to lawyers based on their training in law school, but it can fall flat and come across as defensive to a jury.

After twenty-four years as a courtroom lawyer in private practice I moved in-house and, for fifteen years, was the senior litigation manager for a Fortune 100 company. In that role I had the privilege of working with Litigation Insights. We worked together to develop and test themes to guide the defense teams for three different national mass tort litigations. Trial counsel used those themes to win a number of jury cases, making it possible for the company to resolve each of the mass tort litigations on highly favorable terms.

In this book Merrie Jo Pitera and Barbara Hillmer of Litigation Insights explain what themes are and why they are important. They describe their method for working with defense lawyers to create, test and refine litigation themes that resonate with jurors. They explain the critical importance of developing themes early to guide witness preparation and pretrial discovery. They also give examples of effective ways graphics can be used to reinforce themes and to support the storytelling narrative.

This book is both practical and inspirational. It offers defense lawyers a fresh opportunity to enhance their storytelling skills to create and present emotionally compelling and persuasive courtroom cases.

John Allison, Esq.
Professional Coach and Consultant
The Coach for Lawyers, LLC
www.coachlawyers.com
Former Assistant General Counsel, 3M
Company

SECTION I

NOBODY ROOTS FOR GOLIATH

The problem is plaintiffs have a ready-made underdog story in civil trials: David (their client) against Goliath (your client). Remember, nobody roots for Goliath.

CHAPTER 1

ENTER THE BLACK HAT HIRED GUN PLAINTIFF ATTORNEYS

We are not here to damn all plaintiff attorneys—just some of them.

B eating plaintiff attorneys in a civil trial is a difficult game to win because you are playing against a stacked deck. The best and most effective attorneys are excellent storytellers, and the best plaintiff attorneys often play to jurors' natural distrust of big companies. Our culture has been influenced by decisions like the exploding Ford Pinto or the Pacific Gas and Electric Company's environmental disaster that made a celebrity of Erin Brockovich.

There is a category of plaintiff attorneys, however, that we must recognize beyond the crusading attorneys that have shaped society. We call them the "Black Hat Hired Guns." On the outside they position themselves as knights in shining armor on the scene to save the day. We won't sugarcoat it. Many of these hired gun plaintiff attorneys are opportunistic and profit-motivated by taking advantage of trends to line their pockets. In the end they increase prices, eliminate jobs, and even kill companies.

Do not underestimate the power of these Black Hat Hired Guns. Beating them at their own game is going to be tough because they play games with their own clients, evidence, facts, justice, and their own stories. They do a good job of posing as the champions of the weak and defenseless, while living off settlements and outsized damage awards from companies who find it cheaper to settle than defend.

During the past several decades, we have seen a disturbing trend of these Black Hat Hired Guns winning huge cases against corporations as they preyed upon the biases of jurors, often by playing loose with the facts of a case. A March 2014 *Bloomberg Businessweek* story titled "Judges Slam More and More Plaintiffs' Attorneys for Corruption" captured some of the abuses of plaintiff attorneys, citing cases ranging from a liability verdict against Dole Foods to a multibillion-dollar judgment against Chevron that were thrown out by judges because of plaintiff attorney corruption. The *Businessweek* story defined the fundamental problem defense attorneys face in the legal system: "When you combine these cases with the criminal convictions several years ago of plaintiffs-bar titans Mel Weiss, Bill Lerach, and Dickie Scruggs—all of whom served time for corrupting the civil justice system—it's hard to deny that there's deep dysfunction within a powerful portion of the legal profession that claims to fight corporate abuse on behalf of the little guy."

To be fair, we have to temper the abuses of Black Hat plaintiff attorneys with the stories of legitimate plaintiff attorneys who are fighting the good fight for their clients and who represent the best of the legal profession. The iconic plaintiff attorney Gerry Spence, who was known for wearing a cowboy hat, was a master at persuading juries in complex cases and his work in the late 1970s *Silkwood v. Kerr-McGee Corp.* is a classic example of how plaintiff attorneys can make legal ideas accessible to jurors.

"You'll hear the court tell you about 'strict liability' and it simply means—'If the lion got away, Kerr-McGee has to pay,'" Spence explained to the jurors in the landmark nuclear safety case. "It's that simple. That's the law." Spence persistently hammered home the "lion got away" idea, and the jury awarded the estate of Silkwood $10.5 million for personal injury and punitive damages.

The bottom line is that many defense attorneys need to learn essential lessons from plaintiff attorneys, regardless of the color of their hats or their intentions. And perhaps

the most important lesson is how to overcome the time-tested David v. Goliath story
that plaintiff attorneys present again and
again. The David v. Goliath story all too often
represents the essence of the plaintiff attorneys' strategy—they want to get a panel of
jurors who are sympathetic to the underdog,
and they are committed to portraying the
defense as the privileged bully who has an
unfair advantage.

This is a classic ploy in high-stakes legal bat-
tles, and it can be seen everywhere in the
legal world. We are even seeing big corporations use the tactics of the underdog to persuade jurors. In the ongoing patent disputes
between Apple and Samsung, attorneys for
both sides are constantly refining arguments
and tactics as both of these huge corporations
are, ironically, trying to gain sympathy and
appeal to the emotions of jurors.

According to an April 2014 *New York Times*
story titled "Samsung Executive Says Mar-
keting Drove Phone Sales to No. 1," both

sides are portraying themselves as the wronged little guy: "Apple wants to show how hard the iPhone was to develop before Samsung copied it, while Samsung wants the jury to recognize that catching up to Apple was hard work and that it had to innovate on its own."

All too often, plaintiff attorneys succeed with creating sympathetic themes for jurors as defense attorneys watch helplessly as they are portrayed as the "bad guy." But this doesn't need to be the case.

What do great legendary plaintiff attorneys spanning from Clarence Darrow to William Kunstler have in common? They were all master storytellers, according to legal scholars H. Mitchell Caldwell and Janelle L. Davis, who provide an insightful overview of some of the iconic lawyers of the 20th century in "Timeless Advocacy Lessons from the Masters," published in the *American Journal of Trial Advocacy.*

"Trials cannot be clinical: trials involve flesh and blood individuals frequently caught up in serious, complicated, and dramatic events in which loyalties, loves, hates, lies, prejudices, and the whole spectrum of emotions play a part," Caldwell and Davis observe.

"Jurors, often relying only on emotion, may well climb on board with one of the parties and view events from that vantage point. The masters not only recognize the human drama in every trial, they exploit it to their own success."

Lawyers and jury consultants have been discussing this idea of exploiting the emotional responses of jurors in terms of theories of the brain. Attorney Don Keenan and jury consultant David Ball wrote a 2009 book promoting a theory that plaintiff attorneys often appeal to the reptilian part of the brain, the part of the brain that is emotion-based and can be triggered to overcome reasoned arguments and cause jurors to make decisions that protect themselves and their loved ones. There has been much discussion in the legal world about the validity of this idea of the "reptile brain" in terms of jury communication. But one thing is clear: plaintiff storytelling strategies can encourage jurors to live and decide only in the world of emotions. Defense attorneys must be aware of this tactic and overcome it with a comprehensive narrative that appeals to jurors on many levels.

Defense attorneys must realize that the power of the narrative is not the sole purview of the plaintiff. Our goal is to help defense attorneys understand and reclaim the fundamental value of storytelling in the context of persuading jurors and winning cases.

CHAPTER 2

WHY STORY IS YOUR BEST DEFENSE

*The one who tells the stories rules
the world.*

— NATIVE AMERICAN PROVERB, HOPI TRIBE

A compelling story, not facts or logic alone, is your best defense. Storytelling is primal for humans—in a September 2008 article titled "The Secrets of Storytelling: Why We Love a Good Yarn," *Scientific American* says storytelling is one of the few human traits that is truly universal across cultures and through all of known history. Humans think in stories. From the earliest cave folk who related how they killed a fierce beast to the watercooler stories of today, humans understand facts in context; it helps us make sense of information and aids in memory. People remember the story; they don't remember a recitation of numbers or a list of facts.

Legal scholar Nancy Levit observes in her 2011 article "Reshaping the Narrative Debate" that there has been an evolving trend toward the importance of storytelling in the legal profession. "Two decades ago, a pitched jurisprudential battle surfaced in the pages of law reviews about the value of storytelling as legal scholarship," Levit wrote in the *Seattle University Law Review*. "Since that time, narrative has shifted into academic texts in myriad ways: people are telling stories all over the place. Importantly, also, research is emerging in cognitive neuroscience about the value of stories to human comprehension. And law schools are beginning to consciously recognize that part of what they do is to train storytellers."

This trend is also supported by research in psychology and communication theory that illustrates how central narratives are to human understanding. Because humans think in stories, stories guide the heuristics, or "mental shortcuts," we use. But our previous experiences and attitudes affect how we perceive the story. We "fill in the gaps" of the story according to our existing attitudes, "hear" information that fits with what we already believe, and ignore information that conflicts with those pre-existing beliefs and attitudes. The narratives we create act like filters so that information consistent with what we believe [or our understanding] gets assimilated, and information that is inconsistent is partially or completely ignored.

Any place in the narrative that is unclear or inconsistent creates an ambiguity. And humans don't like ambiguity—most of us feel great pressure to reduce ambiguities or inconsistencies. So it is in those areas of ambiguity that our minds "fill in the blanks" according to what we already think and believe. Ambiguities are particularly ripe areas for cognitive biases to take hold. For example, hindsight bias, or "Monday-morning quarterbacking," allows us to apply the information available today to past events so that outcomes are thus viewed as being predictable. Thus, jurors fill in the gaps with their own biases when making their decisions.

This reality has powerful implications for the courtroom and particularly for communicating with jurors. One may have all the facts and evidence on one's side, but if jurors do not get it, they will reject it and support the other side. If jurors do not understand or believe what you are saying, the case is lost.

At its heart, a trial is an exercise in competing narratives. Both sides are looking at the same set of facts, the same sequence of events. But each has a very different story to tell, based upon those facts. Certain ones are highlighted by the respective sides, and the meaning assigned to facts often differs dramatically. Each side is trying to convince jurors that its version of the facts—its version of the story—is the one jurors should accept. Defense jurors will have a dramatically different story than plaintiff jurors based on how they filter the case stories through their sensibilities.

Understanding the narratives that jurors create is critical because it gives us the opportunity to fill in those gaps in our story and, to the extent necessary, reframe the case facts and themes to best connect with jurors. This understanding also helps us to identify the characteristics of those potential jurors who, because of their pre-existing attitudes and beliefs, would simply be unable to "hear" our story and thus, would be candidates for jury deselection.

We have learned from our research over the years how jurors construct these narratives to help frame the facts and make decisions. Pretrial jury research provides us with a view of competing narratives that are created by jurors in response to the case facts. Now it is time to frame the facts in a story that will carry the day. Where to start? Any good story has certain elements:

- Starting point
- Place
- Characters
- Themes
- Exposition
- Conflict
- Crisis
- Aftermath

Let's start at the very beginning, which may not be the beginning at all. When it comes to the starting point of your narrative (and the defense has a narrative to tell too – the plaintiffs don't get all the fun), consider this: If this case were a movie, what would be Act I, Scene I? Sometimes a good story starts at the beginning, with exposition, followed by conflict, followed by crisis, followed by aftermath. That is traditional storytelling. But sometimes, a story is best told out of order. The movie *Memento* starts at the crisis point and the story is told backward. A more recent film, *The Hangover,* began with the aftermath and the characters were forced to discover the conflict that led to crisis. A case story can start at the beginning, or it may be better to have it start at the point when the plaintiff made a foolish decision that led to the consequences he is now trying to blame on the defense.

Deciding where a story starts makes it easy to create a compelling witness order. Witness order is often an afterthought, subjugated to time constraints and witness availability. Fine courtroom storytellers plot out their stories and carefully plan the witness order to support the story in the sequence in which it is being told.

Place and character development help jurors put themselves in the story—especially "place." Jurors need to understand the time the story took place—if technology and know-how were less developed when the case's key events happened, they need to be taken back to the time when there were no push-button telephones, let alone cell phones.

How do we help jurors remember the story? Our research has shown that the best narratives are reinforced through themes; through simple compelling ideas that are repeated throughout a trial. According to Noah Webster, a theme is "a topic of discourse or discussion, often expressible as a phrase, proposition, or question." Themes are easily remembered, repeatable ideas that bind the story together and give jurors the foundation for arguing on behalf of the defense case.

In some ways, defense lawyers need to think of a case as a great book or movie. We remember enduring novels or films because the writer or director developed compelling characters and themes—from *The Odyssey* to *Hamlet* to *Abaslom! Absalom!* to *Beloved*; from *Gone With the Wind* to *Casablanca* to *Raging Bull* to *Schindler's List*. Like a novelist or a director, successful defense attorneys need to be intentional in the way they craft their storyline and characters.

We are arguing that the best defense teams must combine the traditional elements of preparing for a case—evidence and facts and legal precedents—with a commitment to leveraging the power of a narrative. In the ensuing chapters, we will talk about how we can create specific narratives for jurors that will stay with them as they deliberate a case.

SECTION II

THE EIGHT-STEP PERSUASIVE STORY METHODOLOGY

Knowing that storytelling is important is different than knowing how to tell important stories. While storytelling is thought of as an art, there actually is a great deal of research-based science involved. Based on our successful twenty-year track record, we have developed an eight-step proprietary process for improving connection with jurors and increasing the likelihood of success.

CHAPTER 3

IDENTIFY JURY OBJECTIVES

Perhaps the most important lesson in the art of persuasion, as Aristotle argued more than two thousand years ago, is understanding the needs of your audience.

All too often lawyers fall in love with arguments that they think will work and they lose sight of the context of their case—their goal is to connect with a jury and persuade them to become advocates for their case.

A panel of jurors will ultimately decide your case. Knowing as much as possible about those jurors is, therefore, a critical element of trial strategy. Developing a juror profile requires gathering information about the character-istics of pro-plaintiff/pro-defense jurors in a scientifically valid manner. Just asking staff at your firm or a group of friends what they think doesn't give you reliable information.

We have done extensive research on how ju-rors make decisions and, in many ways, it all goes back to Aristotle's fundamental theory of persuasion. He believed that effective persua-sion must rely on three elements:

- Establishing credibility *(ethos)*

- Making emotional appeals *(pathos)*

- Making rational arguments *(logos)*

In our decades of experience analyzing jurors and how they make decisions, we have seen time and time again that the most successful defense attorneys rely on *ethos, pathos* and *lo-gos* as they work to persuade jurors. And they use these argumentative tactics in the context of a narrative to connect with jurors, to create messages that will resonate with them.

As defense attorneys assess juries and their objectives, they need to keep in mind that humans have limited memory capacity. For example, our ability to remember a string of numbers beyond about seven digits, even on a short-term basis, is limited (hence the seven numbers in a phone number). We also have trouble recalling information we hear only once and thus, repetition is key to our ability to understand and remember. By working through a case story, and by repeating key elements of that story regularly, defense attorneys can help jurors understand and retain information they want them to recall easily throughout trial and deliberations. Those key elements of our story are called "themes."

From a jury psychology perspective, themes are *intentionally oversimplified concepts that connect complex evidence with jurors' experiences, beliefs, and predispositions.* These cognitive "shortcuts" become the cornerstones of the "story of the case"—i.e., an intentionally simplified narrative that enables jurors to distill mountains of complex, ambiguous evidence into a relatively simple, cognitively manageable story that: (1) aligns most closely with their emotional and cognitive predilections; and (2) leaves them feeling that, via their verdict, they have done the right thing.

For litigation themes to serve this function, they must be limited in number and scope and easily repeatable throughout argument and testimony. Although primarily proactive in purpose, good themes should also serve as safe harbors for witnesses during cross examination, offering comfortable framing for uncomfortable questions, especially questions that are highly complex. Finally, although it may seem obvious, it is important to keep in mind that good themes are not a substitute for good evidence and effective testimony; rather, they maximize the impact of good evidence and skilled advocacy.

The dictionary definition of a theme is, *"A topic of discourse or discussion, often ex-*

pressible as a phrase, proposition, or question." Discussion can have themes. Music has themes. Literature has themes. Most importantly, stories have themes. Themes are composed of a few words, a phrase—an easily remembered, easily repeatable statement that jurors can cling to as they strive to organize a mass of new, complicated information that is being thrown at them in a compressed period of time.

When we are constructing themes to simplify a case story for jurors, we can look to a number of sources:

- Story/song titles; and

- Quotes:
    - Famous quotes;
    - Quotes from witnesses; and
    - Quotes from jurors.

We can't overemphasize the value of the last source—quotes from jurors. The defense attorney's objective is to appeal to and persuade jurors. Doesn't it make a world of sense to use themes that are spoken by jurors? Listen to what jurors say in deliberations at a mock trial and/or especially in *voir dire*. When a sitting juror hears words he spoke in *voir dire* reiterated as a theme during trial, he will take ownership of that theme and carry it into the jury room for the defense attorney.

While *voir dire* is often acknowledged as the place to begin asserting your themes, the wise defense attorney will do well to use *voir dire* as a venue in which to *test* themes. People bring their own personal experiences and attitudes to the courtroom and it won't be possible to undo a lifetime of experiences and beliefs over the course of a few days or weeks in court. Highly effective defense attorneys re-tool their thematic framework to fit the beliefs of the jurors. For example, instead of emphasizing the irresponsibility of the plaintiff and coming across as defensive to the jury, counsel may want to look at acknowledging that too many corporations, when faced with important safety decisions, do the wrong thing—but this company is not one of those corporations. Then the thematic emphasis shifts from "Attacking the Plaintiff" to "What the Defendant Did." In order for these pre-disposed jurors to find for your client, they will have to be shown (yes, they place a burden of proof upon you) that your client acted responsibly and did the right thing, and therefore, is different from all those other "bad" corporations.

Our research has also shown that closing arguments are an important persuasive tool. They are the final opportunity to put themes and evidence together in a coherent story. This framing helps jumpstart the jurors' deliberation-room advocacy and provides jurors with an easy-to-remember roadmap for the case right before they transition to deliberation.

The reality is that developing powerful themes throughout the case allows jurors to support your arguments when they are deliberating.

When one juror says in deliberation, "They didn't warn about every possible risk," your jurors need to be able to respond, "Let's talk about 'What the Defendant Did.'" And when another juror says, "This case is just typical of what goes on in corporate America," your jurors can be prepared to respond, "We're here to talk about 'This Case, This Plaintiff.'"

Taking time to create well-developed themes that align with the stories that jurors create as they listen and assimilate will allow you to present your case so that jurors will more effectively digest and recall those themes. In deliberations, the jurors who strongly support your case are your proxy: when they go to do battle on your behalf, those strong themes are their best ammunition.

CHAPTER 4

CONDUCT THE RESEARCH

*Let's move from the idea of big
picture themes to a more pragmatic
but essential element of developing
arguments—jury research.*

Well-designed jury research can help defense attorneys better understand their case and do so from the perspectives of the people who will actually decide the case. Jury research can give the defense insight into how people similar to the actual jury on a case may react to the case's fact pattern and to the success of themes (or the plaintiff attorney's anticipated themes). While research can be done at any phase, the ideal time is early—before witness depositions and before testimony is set in stone so the team has the ability to affirmatively develop the story and case themes. Otherwise, the team can fall into the pattern of trying to make lemonade out of lemons when the testimony is already set.

Jury research is *not* designed to measure the likelihood of victory at trial. One of the cardinal rules of *any* jury research is that it is not designed to be predictive of the ultimate trial outcome. From a methodological standpoint, it's just not possible to design a study that replicates all of the variables that go into a trial; there are just too many things that happen between the test and the trial (e.g., judicial rulings that change the direction of the case, plaintiffs who change their strategy, etc.). Jury research is essential, however, to understanding the beliefs and biases of prospective jurors—a jury profile—and how an array of arguments will affect them.

The most reliable tool to develop a profile is based on the background questionnaire in jury research projects. A background questionnaire is a methodological tool used to assess mock jurors' attitudes, experiences, and demographics. This information is then correlated with jurors' end-of-the-day votes to develop a plaintiff-juror profile for the purpose of jury deselection. That alone makes it an important part of the jury research process. It is the first questionnaire jurors complete when arriving at jury research projects, be it a focus group, mock trial, or deliberation group. It allows the defense team to track jurors' baseline attitudes and experiences before they hear the content of the lawsuit they have been asked to listen to, evaluate, and deliberate to a verdict.

In order to maximize the relevance of a juror profile, it is critical to tailor parts of the background questionnaire to the individual lawsuit that is being tested. Because each case is unique, with its own issues and challenges, having a "one-size-fits-all" questionnaire that includes the same questions for all types of cases won't do the job. Because each juror filters case facts through her own personal predispositions and experiences, it's key to learn what specific factors will impact how she interprets the evidence to develop her narrative of what happened. Therefore, the more general the questionnaire and the wording of its questions, the less likely it is to lead to a refined juror profile that reveals which attitudes and experiences matter most in this case.

Why does the construction of the background questionnaire matter? Because of the effect its results can have on your case, this is not a questionnaire to be taken lightly. It is the foundation of one of the things litigation consultants do—identify the characteristics of the jurors who are strongly predisposed against your case. In order to be able to trust a questionnaire's results, it should be developed according to established research methodology that adheres to appropriate question-and-answer formats. Language used in questions (and answer options, where applicable) needs to accurately capture the attitudes or beliefs you are trying to assess. A question that is poorly worded simply doesn't offer any predictive value. For instance, a double-barreled question (one that assesses two beliefs/concepts at the same time) confounds what you are trying to learn. As a result, this question (and the results that come from it) will lack effectiveness in measuring the attitudes you are trying to identify.

A "plain Jane" questionnaire that gathers demographic information and asks a few general questions cannot delve deeply into jurors' attitudes and beliefs. It is essential to use the right social-science methodology for questionnaire development that is tailored to a specific case. This is the only reliable and valid way to ensure that defense attorneys are obtaining the best foundation for a juror profile.

In addition to developing a focused questionnaire, good research must also take into account demographics. A panel of mock jurors should reflect the demographics and sensibilities of jurors the defense team would see in the actual jurisdiction, anticipating as accurately as possible the effects of hardship excuses and cause strikes on jury composition. This includes recruiting jurors who haven't previously participated in legal research to avoid a response bias. The consequence of having a "veteran" juror means the team could be receiving feedback that the juror *thinks* you want to hear rather than what you *need* to hear. "Virgin" respondents are not familiar with how the process works and therefore, provide feedback not influenced by response bias.

This is critical because the more representative the sample of mock jurors, the more confidence the defense team will have in generalizing results to the larger pool of jury eligibles. And if the goals of the trial team include exploring a potential range of damages and testing themes in an adversarial format, then it is often necessary to include several jury panels in the research in order to ensure reliability and feedback the team can trust.

Jury research is far more than just running a project—it is learning a case and connecting with insights from the people who matter most: representative jurors.

CHAPTER 5

SYNTHESIZE RESEARCH FINDINGS

It is often said that jury research is part art, part science. But make no mistake—there's a significant amount of science in the synthesis of the information gathered in the research process.

As the team analyzes mock juror responses and leanings, they must keep in mind the big picture. The goal is to explain not only *what* happened during the research (reporting of results), but also what the data *means* and how this information can *inform* trial strategy going forward.

Effective jury research must focus on both quantitative and qualitative analysis. It is relatively simple to collect and relay quantitative data—demographics, diachronic juror leanings, or verdict decisions—to the defense team. But what does this quantitative data mean? In the absence of supporting qualitative data, the defense may leave the research exercise with a decent "what," but with no "why." Qualitative data collection, analysis, and synthesis that focus on jurors' reasoning behind their leanings and verdict decisions are essential to a valid and in-depth assessment of the case. This assessment should explore the strengths and vulnerabilities of the case as revealed by juror feedback, along with practical recommendations for themes, story structure, witness order, and strategic guideposts that can be applied at trial. Without this qualitative piece, all the defense team has is a pile of numbers.

A comprehensive analysis of data identifies the key challenges and strengths of a case.

Where does the defense team refine arguments and narratives from here? Generally, these are not purely legal issues, but rather issues of effectively communicating and connecting with jurors. A defense team can have all the facts lined up and on their side, but if the jurors don't understand them or reject the framing of the case, they are likely to reject the defense view and find for the other side. Creating case themes and strategies that leverage psychological and communication principles can help to maximize the defense's story and strengths while minimizing vulnerabilities.

The most valuable component of synthesizing the data in mock-jury exercises is understanding the nuances of jury communication, and it often comes down to language. Qualitative analysis guides the defense team on the right themes, words, and phrases to use and also tells teams which ones to avoid.

Trial teams all too often go into a case with an overarching sense of how they are going to present arguments and which arguments they *think* will work for jurors. Research takes much of the guesswork and reliance on hunches out of the jury communication process, and comprehensive research reveals the specifics of a successful case strategy. A persuasive argument centers on both a big picture sense of narrative as well as a detailed understanding of how targeted themes and language will make jurors advocates for the defense. But if budget precludes a research project, relying on your jury consultant's wealth of knowledge and experience conducting research in your litigation genre is also valuable as you craft your themes.

CHAPTER 6

DEVELOP A PERSUASIVE STORY

What are the building blocks of a persuasive story? In order to persuade, messages should be true to the case goals and easily grasped by a jury, judge, or mediator.

The more messages are aligned with the intended audience, the stronger the case and the better the chances to influence the outcome.

Cases often hinge on witnesses—their opinions and credibility—and the more prepared the witness is with case messages and themes, the better he or she will be able to connect with jurors.

We have all seen the horror stories of witnesses who were unprepared or disengaged. One of the best examples is Bill Gates during the Microsoft antitrust case in the late 1990s. Gates came across as arrogant, detached, and angry, and his testimony clearly hurt the Microsoft defense team. Here's an excerpt from that deposition testimony that exemplifies his evasiveness:

> Q. Did you send this e-mail, Mr. Gates, on or about Aug. 8, 1997?
>
> A. I don't remember sending it.
>
> Q. Do you have any doubt that you sent it?
>
> A. No. It appears to be an e-mail I sent.
>
> Q. You recognize that this is a document produced from Microsoft's files do you not, sir?
>
> A. No.
>
> Q. You don't?

A. Well, how would I know that?

Q. Do you see the document produc-
tion numbers down at the bottom?

A. I have no idea what those numbers
are.

The major problem with the Microsoft case
is that neither Gates nor the defense team
had developed a cohesive story and themes.
They probably believed that Gates was smart
enough to address any questioning by the
plaintiff lawyers, and this proved to be a strategic flaw. The very qualities that made Gates
and Microsoft so successful—supreme confidence and willful independence—came back
to haunt the company in the antitrust lawsuit.

As early as discovery, and prior to being de-
posed by plaintiff counsel, both expert and
fact witnesses can be given tools (thematic
responses) to deal with tough questions that
are designed to perpetuate the perceived vulnerabilities of the defense case. Knowledge of
these common plaintiff framings can inform

and shape the deposition process. They can also uncover counter-themes that directly contradict plaintiff juror predispositions while arming defense jurors with arguments of their own to take into the jury room. Successful defense teams work with their witnesses to help them organize their testimony and develop their thematic points. They know that well-prepared witnesses are the absolute key for credibility in the minds of jurors. How witnesses present themselves, how they make eye contact, how they dress—these are all essential to jury communication.

Through our years of experience, we have identified some guidelines for defense teams to help witnesses be at the top of their game:

Watch, listen and learn. What are your witnesses saying, how are they saying it, and does it fit with your case theme?

Educate and involve. Fill your witnesses in on trial strategy and themes. Make sure they understand what you're trying to get done and where pitfalls may lie. Show them the verbal and non-verbal behaviors that can increase or decrease credibility for jurors.

Evaluate and improve. Provide detailed feedback on a practice run of their testimony. Help them use economy in words and body language.

Perhaps the best way to think about a compelling story is to start with the characters, and the primary characters to convey the story are witnesses. Witnesses can be difficult. They can sometimes come across as harsh, arrogant, evasive—even unlikable and unbelievable. Providing sworn testimony is stressful, and developing well-prepared witnesses with the skills to communicate their knowledge in a way that easily informs and ultimately helps persuade judges, juries, and arbitration panels is essential to the success of the defense team.

The best defense teams view a case in many ways like a book, where they have a clear sense of the development of the story and they know the ending. They build on the facts of the case and their growing understanding of compelling arguments. At the same time, effective defense teams learn lessons from the best public affairs or political machines: they create messages that they know will resonate with their audience and they stay on message. Everyone in the trial knows these messages—witnesses, attorneys, paralegals, support staff, jury research consultants, trial graphics experts . . . the list goes on. And they all communicate these messages in a variety of ways.

There's a reason random slogans or advertising jingles stay in our heads for decades.

- Coke, it's the real thing.

- The happiest place on earth.

- Keeps going and going and going.

- Thanks, I needed that.

- Put a Tiger in your tank.

- Just do it.

It's all about repetition and simplicity. A trial generally doesn't last as long as an advertising campaign, but in the condensed time frame of a trial the defense team can use key phrases consistently to get the same effect—the repeated words and ideas will stay in the minds of jurors as they deliberate.

Inevitably, trials have unexpected turns and defense teams must be nimble in addressing changing tactics in the course of a trial. The key to developing a persuasive story, however, is the consistency of messaging—using the same phrases, the same ideas over and over again.

A winning, persuasive strategy has all of the players working together seamlessly, and they have a clear sense of themes even during the most difficult and stressful times in a trial. A good attorney or a good witness has the ability to handle many types of questions and support a trial theme at the same time. They are confident and can easily adapt to the ebb and flow of testimony while holding fast to the message they need to communicate.

CHAPTER 7

PREPARE MEMORABLE GRAPHICS

Compelling trial graphics can unify the defense team's presentation and drive home the most important themes. Graphics are powerful tools because they often have the ability to communicate more clearly and concisely than words.

E very graphic should communicate a theme. That is, developing graphics can impose discipline on the trial team—both lawyers and client—by forcing them to focus on themes. Ideally, making these choices early in litigation can help all team members pull on the same side of the rope and avoid the unpleasant "Why are we arguing that?" conversation with the client on the eve of trial.

Trial graphics can be used as outlines for discovery, especially in recurring litigation. If you know what data you will need to build out your graphics in an individual case, you can focus more clearly on developing those data in discovery. Along the same lines, if multiple lawyers or law firms will be taking depositions around the country, preliminary trial graphics can serve as educational materials to ensure that attorneys and witnesses are focusing on information essential to the development of themes and graphics. Such guidance can be especially important with experts; if you know what scientific evidence or failings you want to show to the jury, you can be sure to gather the necessary testimony and documents in discovery.

Graphics also provide essential ways to sharpen arguments and storylines during jury research. If the goal of a mock trial is to test your vulnerabilities as well as your case themes, you should also spend some time developing graphics for the opposing side. This balanced approach will allow mock jurors to weigh the arguments equally. Additionally, a mock trial allows the time to rehearse opening and closing presentations and provides a less stressful training ground for the attorneys to present their graphics in front of the jury.

All lawyers have had the experience of thinking they've identified a winning argument, only to have it fall apart when they say it out loud. It sounded good in your head, but it sounded ridiculous (or mean, or too complicated) when you spoke the words. Developing graphics requires you to go a step further, turning concepts into images the entire trial team can see, hear, and understand. Arguments that survive the transition from thought to concrete image are more likely to persuade at trial.

An integrated graphic approach to storytelling can add simplicity to complex concepts and make a case come alive for jurors. Following are tried and true graphics elements that can engage jurors and reinforce fundamental themes for the defense:

The timeline. Giving jurors a clear understanding of the sequence of events and their proximity in time is critical. A timeline can also be a devastating tool for impeachment by showing clearly how and when a witness reversed field. In any case, it's important to introduce each event one by one rather than all at once, even if you are running short on time.

The checklist. Because jurors likely use checklists in their daily lives, using this tool to list and check off important pieces of evidence is familiar to them. It can also focus your witness or help control opposing witnesses.

The bar graph. These types of graphics have been around forever, and there's a good reason why—they are easy to understand. Today's bar graphs use 3D elements and gradient colors to convey different characteristics of the data being presented and are particularly useful for illustrating comparisons and trends.

The transcript. Slides showing text from witness testimony don't have to simply show a scan of the transcript. Instead, use a photograph of the witness, take the time to bold questions or answers, or animate each question and answer one by one. Using this tool during closing argument allows you to drive home points most relevant to your arguments and case themes.

The organizational chart. Showing how an entity is organized (e.g., a company, government agency) is much more effective and efficient if done graphically.

Summary slides. In closing arguments, summary slides remind your jurors what they have learned about the case. Simple, memorable summary slides—often comprised of memorable icons and bulleted lists—may provide jurors who are leaning your direction with talking points to use in the jury room.

Most of the above elements are focused on electronic graphics that are created and displayed on a computer. The days of foregoing electronic graphics, because you don't want to come across as too corporate and slick, are over. In an age when virtually every elementary school student can use PowerPoint or iMovie, failing to use electronic graphics will just make you look dated. Besides, jurors expect it and not meeting their expectations could leave you looking unprepared. That said, don't forget the role non-electronic demonstratives can play.

Using the ELMO document camera to display documents, particularly on cross-examination or re-direct where unexpected testimony has raised a new issue, can help break up the presentation. Even lower-tech solutions, such as flip charts and foam boards, can still be very effective. These media have the advantage of permanence (i.e., while your electronic graphics will vanish when opposing counsel stands up, a flip chart listing key points can be left facing the jury even after you sit down). Moreover, if opposing counsel does not want the jury looking at the flip chart, he has to either turn it himself or ask the Court to have you take it down. Either way, your opponent has to deal with your chart—and perhaps look as if it contains facts they want to hide.

The approach to using graphics *well* requires a team effort. The following tips for developing graphics can significantly improve your presentation and arguments during trial:

> ***Hire a dedicated trial presentation technician.*** Few, if any, lawyers are better at running graphics than a trained trial presentation professional. Moreover, a trial lawyer's brainpower should not be focused on cueing up the next video or slideshow.

Create graphics to be modular. Break your graphics into pieces that can be swapped out or deleted based on rulings at trial. No matter what you promise your client, you can't predict a trial judge's ruling with regard to any piece of evidence. Your graphics must, therefore, be constructed so that controversial topics or pieces of evidence can be removed immediately before opening or just as your primary witness is taking the stand. This is why PowerPoint is very functional at trial. Your presentation technician, who is thoroughly familiar with your graphics, can remove or edit Power-Point slides on demand. Foam boards can't be fixed so quickly.

Tailor graphics to your witnesses. If you have an expert witness with communication challenges, design your graphics to compensate for his or her particular weaknesses. For example, if your witness has a challenging accent, make sure your graphics highlight critical words or phrases that the jury may not be able to get from his testimony. If the witness has difficulty staying on topic, use bulleted lists to keep him or her focused. On the contrary, if you are lucky enough to have a charismatic witness with a strong and pleasing voice, use graphics only for the points you truly wish to hammer.

Rehearse your presentation in its entirety. Regardless of what graphics you use and who runs the computer, it's essential to test your full presentation. For example, if you have a timeline with multiple linked events and documents, practice the presentation on the computer that you will use in the courtroom. Minor differences in installed fonts and software settings can cause your presentation to lose polish in front of the jury. And, a lawyer who looks at the display screen more than the jury is a lawyer who needs more rehearsal time.

While graphics wield great power in communicating themes to juries, it's essential to remember that you, not the graphics, are the storyteller. The graphics are there to help guide you and your audience through your story.

CHAPTER 8

INTEGRATE STORY STRATEGY

Great storytellers use an array of tactics to engage their audience. They appeal to reason and emotion to connect with the audience. They rely on the credibility and believability of the characters in a story. As the defense team works to develop its story strategy, it must integrate all of these persuasion approaches to connect with jurors.

All too often, we see lawyers who fall into the trap of believing that evidence and arguments are enough to prevail in a case. They don't realize that the overarching story and themes—*supported by evidence and arguments*—are the keys to winning a case.

Creating a cohesive narrative and themes also addresses a fundamental challenge in real trials—information often comes to jurors in a non-sequential manner. Witnesses are not called from the beginning of a legal issue to the end, and trials frequently take unanticipated turns. Without an intentional, cohesive story and themes to tie a case together, jurors are often left with a bunch of pieces of evidence that they can't make sense of, so they tend to ignore the evidence.

So how does the defense team integrate its story strategy and themes into the case? During jury research, the team tests different persuasive tactics and arguments with mock jurors. The defense goal is clear: to appeal to and persuade jurors. Doesn't it make sense, therefore, to use themes that are spoken by jurors? Listen to what jurors say in deliberations at a mock trial or in *voir dire* at trial and use those words to create your story.

As the defense integrates its story, it needs to use a wide range of tactics to grab the attention of jurors and keep them engaged. Jurors all need to hear, understand, and remember the same message, even when filtered through their personal interests, beliefs, and biases. Here are some basic rules we employ to effectively communicate with jurors:

> ***Keep it simple. Boil it down.*** The imprint value of a message is inversely related to its complexity. Keep circling back to your themes as you present your evidence. Consider a small number of mounted presentation boards on easels to reinforce these themes.

> ***Titles are huge thematic reinforcement opportunities.*** Titles should pose a question, make a statement, or reinforce a theme. "Timeline," "Personal History," or "Chronology of Events" are useless titles and waste one of your best opportunities for imprinting themes and posing ques-

tions. Don't identify the type of graphic; tell the jury what it means!

Test your presentations before you complete them. This is the best confidence builder for new presentations. Showcase your work-in-progress presentation to people not completely familiar with the topics and/or content of your case to measure communication effectiveness. Fold this input into your final drafts.

Start using these themes refined and/or derived from jury research as early as *voir dire*, if permitted, when you first come into contact with jurors. This provides the defense team with several opportunities to prime jurors to the defense themes, to test the themes with the panel and assess reactions.

Moving from *voir dire* to the heart of the trial, make sure that defense witnesses clearly articulate themes during their testimony. Themes help jurors connect what the witness is saying with the overall case, and understanding the case themes helps the witness with his or her role in the overall story that is being presented at trial. Equally important, themes become a safe harbor for witnesses during intense cross examination; they can come back to their main thematic points when being pressed by opposing counsel.

We have all seen cases when the witnesses deliver testimony that is highly scripted. Sounding pat and over-prepared adversely affects a witness's credibility. Jurors have told us in post-trial interviews (and in our mock trials) that an over-prepared or scripted witness loses credibility because they are "saying what they have been told to say."

It is extremely important to run witnesses through their direct and anticipated cross to help refresh the witness regarding the facts and themes of his or her testimony. The trick is to work to preserve some semblance of extemporaneous delivery for the final performance—the one in the courtroom.

Once the trial begins, the defense themes should be apparent in every facet of the case—from opening statements to closings. But the true time when themes are most important is after the defense team sits down for the last time and the jury heads to deliberate the case—true persuasion comes during input and discussion with fellow jurors. It is critical that jurors who support the defense case understand your themes so they can use them to argue for your position during these deliberations.

In the real world of civil trials and deliberations, we still see this scenario happen consistently. Jurors who are influenced by powerful and consistent defense themes can become tireless advocates for your case, swaying fellow jurors and delivering the verdict that the defense wants. That is the reward for crafting and developing an integrated narrative that connects with, and persuades, jurors on multiple levels.

CHAPTER 9

IDENTIFY THE JURORS YOU DON'T WANT

Most veteran trial lawyers will agree that while a case is not won in jury selection, it can certainly be lost there.

Voir dire is one of the three most critical junctures of any trial, yet it is usually relegated to the proverbial back burner, only attended to in the waning days—or even hours—before trial begins. For those who wait until the last moment to prepare for jury selection, the outcomes are often disappointing. Those who plan for this vital element of a trial invariably have an edge.

It may sound surprising, but *voir dire* development should begin as early as the pretrial jury research phase, when the defense and research teams have presented case arguments and stories to mock jurors and received feedback on the issues. From the outset, the defense team must assess what attitudinal and experiential factors were most important in distinguishing the strongest pro-defense jurors from their pro-plaintiff counterparts. As the defense develops case themes and storylines, it can start listing potential bias issues that may prevent certain jurors from being persuaded by the defense case. It is easy to prioritize opening, closing, or preparation of motions over *voir dire*; however, the long hours devoted to these other important aspects of trial could be for naught if the most dangerous jurors for the case are overlooked during *voir dire*.

"Who do I want on this jury?" we often hear. Wrong question.

The better question must be: "Who *don't* I want?" The first objective of a good *voir dire* is to identify jurors who are fundamentally predisposed against the defense case, who don't have the ability to hear the defense story. The second objective of a good *voir dire* is to get those jurors to talk. The third objective is to get those risky jurors to talk themselves off the panel.

There are secondary objectives of *voir dire*, as well: to prime the jurors with case themes and get jurors talking about them during the jury selection process and to gain commitments that the defense can return to during closing arguments ("You'll remember that before we started this trial, each of you promised to hold the plaintiff to his burden of proof...").

So, what are the key strategies to putting forth an effective *voir dire* and jury de-selection for the client? Two words: *planning* and *practice*.

The construction of *voir dire* needs to start weeks before the case gets to trial, after the defense has conducted pretrial research. Virtually no practicing trial attorney goes into the beginning of trial without practicing his or her opening statement. In the past, however, very few trial attorneys have practiced *voir dire*, the part of the trial when they speak to jurors first. What we are seeing now, however, is that more attorneys are choosing to do some formal *voir dire* practice in advance of trial. Most often that practice takes the form of a *voir dire* focus group and during *voir dire* in the mock trial. Below are several benefits to be derived from taking the time to test your *voir dire* in advance of trial:

> **There is no rush.** Working on an outline/ question list for a *voir dire* focus group can enhance preparation for this key event and reduce last-minute rushing.

> **Vet your questions.** This benefit is especially important if the *voir dire* time is going to be limited by the judge. *Voir dire* focus groups allow the defense to find out in advance which questions are most im-

portant and which ones best identify your riskiest jurors.

Refine the questions you will use. Part of the purpose of the *voir dire* focus group is to get direct feedback regarding the participants' experiences. This feedback can help you avoid pitfalls at trial, such as impromptu jokes that fall flat, such as saying to a jury panel, "Those who can, do; those who can't, teach," thereby offending every single juror with a teacher in their family.

Work on the "close-out" technique to get individuals to admit biases and thereby reveal themselves as eligible for a cause strike. The *voir dire* focus group is the place to make mistakes in cultivating a cause strike and to perfect the technique before trial. A good for-cause questioning technique is one of the most valuable skills to preserve peremptory strikes and remove even more jurors who are biased against the case.

Practice can help put you at ease in front of the panel. It is important in *voir dire* to be spontaneous, accessible, and tuned in to the prospective jurors. The attorney who has practiced his *voir dire* will find it easier to get "off script" and just be with the jurors, making for a more productive session in which jurors talk more— and reveal more.

The great thing about doing such a focus group is that it can be conducted in two to three hours—start to finish. Juror recruitment is somewhat less formal than for a mock trial or deliberation group, and thus is more economical. And the relatively low cost of the event makes for a potentially terrific return on investment. Typically, twelve to fifteen jurors participate in the exercise. Upon arrival, they simply fill out a background questionnaire and listen to a brief orientation by a consultant. Focus group jurors participate in a mock *voir dire* that lasts approximately one to two hours. The focus group allows jurors to provide feedback through their responses to questions about whether they felt comfortable and safe in sharing their views, what questions resonated with them and what else the attorney could have asked to draw out more responses.

Just like a good wine, *voir dire* development also takes time—the best questions mature with practice and focus. Knowing what works early on, and polishing those questions so they better identify risks, will produce the best results in *voir dire*, when it really matters.

CHAPTER 10

ASSESS STORY EFFECTIVENESS

Few resources offer more valuable information than post-trial interviews with jurors who just decided the case. These post-trial interviews are especially beneficial in situations where litigation of a similar type or with similar themes is expected in the future.

The feedback jurors provide can include their reactions to key themes, arguments, witnesses, graphics, demonstratives, and even evaluations of each side's presenting attorneys. In essence, these trial jurors are the ultimate focus group, appraising how the information was presented and, more importantly, how it was understood and discussed in the deliberation room. This provides a window into how the group reached its ultimate verdict.

And yet, interviewing jurors post-trial can also have adverse consequences. Consider the following: In 2010, a Florida attorney was sentenced to six-month's jail time for contacting a former juror without the consent of the court. In fact, such contact has been highly controversial since the 1978 case of *United States v. Sherman*. In this case, the judge declared that such juror contact might interfere with defendants' sixth amendment right to a fair trial and jurors' right to be protected from harassment. The appeals court, however, disagreed and permitted the interviews. In subsequent cases, judges have allowed post-trial interviews—sometimes with certain restrictions—or have prevented them from occurring entirely.

Due to the disparate rules throughout our court system, juror interviews can be fraught with challenges, turning a potential gold mine of valuable information into a potential minefield. The following are some simple guidelines for conducting successful post-trial interviews:

Secure permission. Before beginning the interview process, be sure to receive the judge's consent. This protects you should any issues arise from such conduct or contact. Similarly, ask the judge to advise jurors that they can discuss the case with others once a verdict is reached. Often, jurors question whether they are even allowed to talk to the trial team and the trial consultants following a verdict. Rather than leaving jurors to wonder, it is advisable that the judge inform them of the rules ahead of time.

Never pressure a juror to talk. This may seem like a simple rule, but it is often overlooked. Given the emotion and excitement after trial, it is understandable that an attorney would want to garner as much information from jurors as quickly as possible—but some jurors may not wish to reciprocate. One way to make jurors more comfortable is by telling them that they do not have to answer any questions that make them uncomfortable and that they can stop the interview at anytime. This puts the ball in their court. And if you get a sense that a juror is still uncomfortable, back off.

Establish rapport. Obviously, there are a multitude of reasons to connect with your jurors; one is that after trial they will be more apt to answer your lingering questions. If your goal is to simply talk to a handful of jurors for a few minutes, they will be more likely to talk to you if they feel a personal rapport or connection with you. This connection can be established as early as *voir dire*, and the more you build that connection, the more likely it is they will talk to you once trial is over.

Work with a third party. The benefits
of using a third party to conduct post-trial interviews include their ability to elicit candid opinions—the kind that jurors may not feel comfortable sharing when face-to-face with the actual attorneys. One suggestion for more comprehensive interviews is to use a consulting firm with consultants who are trained in social-science-based research and interviewing techniques. For example, we work in collaboration with the trial team to formulate an interview guide that ensures the necessary information is gleaned in accordance with the trial team's goals, and questions are asked in a way that avoids inadvertently leading the jurors. Additionally, a good consulting firm will save you time because they possess an established interview protocol and methods for obtaining juror contact information.

Don't forget the logistics. When will you call the jurors? It's important to be cognizant of job schedules. If you expect to reach people during standard nine-to-five business hours, you will be disappointed. How long will the interviews take? Some jurors perceive these interviews as an imposition, especially if they were seated on a lengthy trial. In recognition that their time and opinions are valuable, some interviewers offer them an incentive to participate. What is the best use of time for you and the juror? Given the limited amount of time most people have to participate in an interview, it is sometimes best to ask a smaller number of your most important questions than attempting to ask a large amount of questions. Additionally, asking open-ended questions is more likely to result in meaningful insight than asking questions that can merely be answered with a "yes" or "no."

The quest to find the rationale in the vast area between yes and no, between negligent and not negligent, is particularly important in preparing the defense team for possible appeals. Post-trial interviews reveal the mindset of jurors in a specific case—the conversation between attorneys and jurors can give the defense a clear sense of winning, as well as losing arguments, and provides a roadmap for developing future themes and stories for the case.

Post-trial individual juror interviews bring understanding and clarity on how decisions are made. Whether it's good news or bad news, the defense needs to know how and why a verdict was reached. Interviews validate and reinforce good strategies and techniques, and ensure that you will avoid less effective ones in the future. And it's essential to capture these impressions immediately after a verdict. The key is to ask jurors specifically which components of the presented themes and arguments resonated with them and get them to open up and be frank about their attitudes and opinions. This method is powerful for isolating individual interpretations, bias, and reactions.

Our research has shown that individual thoughts and feelings change in group settings. As an alternative to the individual interview, we also work to reconvene as many jurors as possible for a group discussion. Through this process, the defense team can gain valuable insight into jurors' decision rationale, including reactions to key arguments, witness testimony and demonstratives. The key is to look for patterns in individual thinking and compare those to the collective decision-making process and outcome. Persuasion within the group becomes the focus and it's important to see how those dynamics play out.

SECTION III

THE POWER OF IMPROVED JURY CONNECTION

Taking time to create well-developed themes that align with jurors' stories will allow you to present your case so that jurors can remember and understand your story.

CHAPTER 11

THE END OF THE STORY

Tell 'em what you're going to tell 'em.
Tell 'em.
Tell 'em what you told them.
Sit Down.

— An old trial truism that isn't very true

Traditional narrative has a beginning, a middle, and an end. The end of the story is very important; we all want to know how the story ends. Does our hero get the girl? Does our heroine survive the killer storm? Do they live happily ever after?

There are a few internal issues at play for jurors by the time the defense lawyer gets up to deliver closing arguments:

- Most of them *believe* they know how they feel about the case.

- Most of them are eager to talk about the case.

- Many of them are experiencing some level of anxiety and/or confusion over what they are being asked to do by the parties.

But it is not during closing arguments that those internal issues get resolved—it is during deliberations. A meta-analysis conducted by Litigation Insights of 1,631 jurors who participated in mock trials between January 1, 2011, and June 22, 2012, showed that 53.6 percent of jurors changed their leaning—toward plaintiff or defense—during deliberations. A full eighty-five percent of undecided jurors waited until deliberations—not closings—to finally make up their minds.

If the persuasion is happening in the jury room, and not during closing, what is the purpose of closing argument? It's simple: help jurors put the fitting end to the story by helping them understand the job that is before them and arming those jurors who are sympathetic to the defense case with the words and ideas they need to counter the objections of plaintiff-leaning jurors.

When you begin to put your closing together, think in terms of "What is going to happen next?" What is going to happen is this—twelve relative strangers are going into a small room to discuss, argue, barter, and compromise. They need help. Give jurors that help by arming them for argument by predicting the future. Ultimately, the goal of the defense team is to walk the jurors through the strange process that they are about to embark upon and ease their anxiety about it.

By the time an attorney gets up to close, the panel of jurors has heard enough. They've listened to arguments, details, theories, and to witness upon witness. And they've made some judgments along the way. They want to talk about the case already, and in some ways they perceive the closing oratory as an obstacle to getting to do that. Before the defense team can accomplish anything in closing, you first have to give them a reason to listen to you. One way to do that is to predict the future: "When you go back into that jury room, you are going to have two jobs," you can begin. "Your first job is going to be to answer the questions that the court wants you to answer. Your second job will be to explain to your fellow jurors why you feel the way you do about each of the issues those questions raise." Now they have a reason to listen.

The true job of the jurors—answering the verdict form—often gets relegated to a few minutes at the end of closing. It is so very critical to help the jurors understand how to deliberate. If you are in a venue that allows you to do so, start with the instructions. If there are terms in the instructions that routinely confuse laypeople (e.g., "preponderance," "proximate cause"), explain them in laymen's terms. What does an instruction on "Agency" or "Scope of Employment" mean? Then, walk them through the verdict form; if one question is predicated on another, make sure jurors are clear on that. Take the time now to refer back to the evidence in the case and apply it—not rhetorically, but concretely—to the very questions they are being called upon to answer. And make sure they understand which instructions apply to which questions on the verdict form. Attorneys make the mistake of assuming that legal constructs that seem logical to someone who spent three years in law school will seem equally logical to laypeople. It all comes back to persuasion and focusing on the needs of your audience. The closing argument represents the last time that an attorney can pinpoint questions that jurors might have about the case and provide them with an easy path to resolve those questions.

The closing allows the defense attorney to take on the role of facilitator—a person who understands the difficulty and the emotion of the job that jurors will be called upon to do. In the role of facilitator, the defense can increase credibility as you provide clarity for your triers of fact. More than anything, clarity is what jurors need at the end of a trial as the story draws to a close. Not convention. Not self-indulgence. Clarity. It is no longer about you or about your client. It is now about the jurors and the job they are about to do. Ask yourself, "How can I make this upcoming process as clear as possible for them?" Clear thoughts produce clear results.

The effective closing argument is rarely the dramatic monologue that we see in *Law and Order* or the heroic attorney movie of the day. The nuance and power of the defense narrative has already been told and explained to jurors well before the closing. The closing reiterates those themes efficiently and clearly before jurors head off to deliberate the case.

CHAPTER 12

THE STORYTELLING MINDSET

We have focused in this book on storytelling in the context of trials and persuading jurors. But the lessons of developing great stories and themes can be learned well beyond the legal world.

T here is an increasing emphasis on the importance of narrative and storytelling in a wide range of fields. A July 2014 *Harvard Business Review* articled titled "How to Tell a Great Story" captured the ubiquitous influence and relevance of good storytelling:

"We tell stories to our coworkers and peers all the time—to persuade someone to support our project, to explain to an employee how he might improve, or to inspire a team that is facing challenges. It's an essential skill, but what makes a compelling story in a business context? And how can you improve your ability to tell stories that persuade?" the *HBR* article asks. "Fortunately, everyone has the ability to become a better storyteller. 'We are programmed through our evolutionary biology to be both consumers and creators of story,' says Jonah Sachs, CEO of Free Range Studios and author of *Winning the Story Wars*. 'It certainly can be taught and learned.'"

One of the key elements to successful storytelling that we have explored is the fundamental importance of understanding the needs of your audience. All too often in trials attorneys think they are talking to people just like them, people with the same education, background and expertise on a given case. Or the legal team gets caught up in the business politics of a trial and thinks that they need to make arguments that will be palatable or resonant with the CEO of the company they are defending.

When this happens, they lose the sense of the character of the audience that matters most—twelve people from very different backgrounds who have come together to hear competing arguments and themes in a case. They are twelve people who yearn to hear complex ideas conveyed in language that is clear and compelling. They are twelve people who are eager to hear a story that makes sense and engages them.

The best defense teams should take their cues from successful storytellers all around them. When they read great novels or works of nonfiction, they should remember why they were drawn to those books. When they see the rare really—good movie, they should learn about the importance of character development and how a good movie always leaves the audience with an ending that is authentic and believable.

When it all comes down to it, good lawyers are teachers who tell stories to jurors in order to inform them and fill in knowledge gaps. When you read the transcript of a superb trial lawyer in an intellectual property case, for example, you see an attorney who is able to break down complex concepts for a panel of jurors using simple, effective language. You see a teacher who is helping a jury understand at once his client's business model and who, at the same time, is connecting the various themes of a story to create advocates when the jurors are deliberating the case.

We always remind defense lawyers to focus on one question: What story do you want to tell? Don't focus on the story the plaintiff is trying to tell—always focus on your story and how you are going to keep jurors on your side of the house. Or think of it this way: If you had to tell someone at a dinner party about your case, what story would you tell about your side of it? We all think in stories, especially those sitting in the jury box. Jurors want to know what happened between these opposing parties that landed them in court, not a list of evidence and complex facts. Instead, tell a story that answers jurors' questions about motives for the lawsuit and the significance of your case, which should simplify the complexity. Talking in stories makes your complex litigation more jury-friendly.

There's a saying that goes, "What you focus on expands." Ultimately, the key to helping jurors understand your complicated case lies in focusing not on its complexity, but on its simplicity.

ABOUT THE AUTHORS

Merrie Jo Pitera, Ph.D.

Merrie Jo Pitera is a psychology and communications expert who specializes in complex litigation and trial consulting and is the CEO of Litigation Insights, a full-service trial consulting firm headquartered in Kansas City. She has more than twenty-five years of experience in the field and focuses on helping clients perform at their highest levels. She has managed hundreds of cases during her career, and as a result, understands what's at stake and knows how to help clients build persuasive themes.

As one of the leading trial consultants in the country, Dr. Pitera is a perceptive listener and observer of jury dynamics and sentiments and provides clear insights into how they are likely to impact a case. In addition to being a jury specialist, she also prepares witnesses for depositions, trials and congressional hearings. She is a frequent national and international speaker on jury behavior and witness prep methods and routinely publishes articles on witness preparation, jury selection and trial preparation. In addition, she is one of the leading experts on hindsight bias in the courtroom, most specifically reducing jurors' tendency to engage in hindsight.

In the more than ten years Dr. Pitera has been CEO/Managing Partner of Litigation Insights, the company has grown to include among its clients fifty-three Fortune 500 companies and many of the leading legal firms in the country. In 2010, she was selected as one of the "Women Who Mean Business" by the *Kansas City Business Journal* for her leadership role at Litigation Insights and within the community.

Barbara Hillmer, Ph.D.

Barbara Hillmer has more than twenty-five years of experience in research, consulting and case management, working with clients to help them achieve their goals. She is particularly skilled at interpreting quantitative and qualitative data to analyze cases from jurors' perspectives and structuring thematic narratives that appeal to jurors' sensibilities. She works to help clients understand the importance of stories in communicating effectively with jurors.

Dr. Hillmer's research focus has included a wide range of matters including employment, banking, financial services, product liability, and financial and securities litigation, as well as environmental litigation. Her background in communication and group dynamics allows her to develop persuasive case themes and strategies that connect with jurors. In particular, her work in understanding and appealing to the perspectives of one's audience, built upon principles based on psychology, rhetoric and the cognitive sciences, have been important in reinforcing the narrative underpinnings of effectively communicating with jurors.

Prior to joining Litigation Insights, she conducted applied research as a management consultant for companies, including the Sprint Corporation, where she focused on effective communication in human resources and management. A certified mediator, Dr. Hillmer has also conducted research in assessing and managing conflict in organizations. In addition, she has numerous publications and presentations addressing how stories and themes are essential to effective communication.

Made in the USA
Monee, IL
23 February 2023

28520074R00069